GEOGRAPHY

FACTS

FOR SHARP MINDS

A wonderful book for the whole Family!

INTRODUCTION

Geography is the study of the world around us, from the physical features of the Earth to the ways in which humans interact with and shape their environment. It is a vast and fascinating subject that encompasses everything from the tiniest microbes to the most prominent mountain ranges, and from the most remote and inhospitable regions of the planet to the bustling metropolises that are home to millions of people.

This book will explore some of the most exciting and surprising facts about geography, from the deepest parts of the ocean to the highest peaks of the world's tallest mountains. We will delve into the mysteries of the Earth's natural wonders, such as the Great Barrier Reef and the Grand Canyon, and learn about the incredible diversity of planet Earth.

As we delve into the pages of this book, we will discover how human activity has influenced and molded the planet throughout history. From the ancient civilizations that constructed magnificent cities to the contemporary world, each piece of information will provide a more profound understanding of the intricacy and magnificence of our planet, leaving us in awe of the wonders of the world around us.

Canada has more lakes in the world than any other country.

According to estimates, Canada boasts an impressive number of 31,752 lakes, each larger than 3 square kilometers. This number surpasses that of any other country globally, making Canada a true lake paradise. These lakes span across Canada's vast landmass, covering approximately 9% of the country's total land area. This means that you can travel through much of Canada and come across a lake at every turn. From the deep blue waters of Lake Louise to the crystal-clear waters of Moraine Lake, Canada's lakes are breathtakingly beautiful and offer a wide range of recreational activities, from swimming to boating and fishing. Other countries with significant numbers of lakes include Finland, Russia, and the United States.

Mount Everest, located in the Himalayas, is the highest peak on Earth.

It is standing at 8,848 meters (29,029 feet) above sea level. It is located on the border between Nepal and Tibet and has two main climbing routes, the South Col route in Nepal and the North Col route in Tibet. Climbing Mount Everest is considered a challenging and dangerous feat, and only experienced climbers attempt it. Despite the risks involved, thousands of people attempt to climb Mount Everest each year. The official height of Mount Everest was determined in 2020 by a joint team of Nepali and Chinese surveyors, and its height continues to be a subject of fascination and scientific study. It was named after Sir George Everest, a British surveyor who was responsible for surveying much of India, including the Himalayas.

The largest hot desert in the world is located in Africa.

The Sahara Desert in Africa is the largest hot desert in the world, spanning 3.6 million square miles. The Sahara is located across Northern Africa and is roughly the size of the United States. It is known for its hot, arid climate, and has recorded some of the highest temperatures on Earth, with the hottest temperature ever recorded being 136°F (57.8°C) in Libya. Despite the harsh conditions, the Sahara is home to a variety of plant and animal species, including camels, gazelles, and desert hyenas. The Sahara has a rich cultural history and has been home to various civilizations, such as the ancient Egyptians and the Tuareg people, who are known for their distinctive blue clothing.

Fact# 4

The lowest point on Earth.

The Dead Sea, located between Israel and Jordan, is the lowest point on Earth, sitting at 427 meters (1,401 feet) below sea level. The Dead Sea is a saltwater lake bordered by Jordan to the east and Israel to the west. It is known for its high salt concentration, which is nearly ten times that of the world's oceans, and makes it impossible for most forms of marine life to survive in it. However, the Dead Sea is a popular tourist destination because its high salt and mineral content is believed to have therapeutic benefits for skin and joint problems. The Dead Sea has a rich history, and its shores are home to several biblical sites, including the ancient city of Jericho and the Qumran Caves, where the Dead Sea Scrolls were discovered.

The world's largest coral reef system is stretched over 1,400 miles.

Great Barrier Reef in Australia is the world's largest coral reef system. The Great Barrier Reef is made up of over 2,900 individual reefs and is home to thousands of species of fish, marine mammals, and other marine life. It is also one of the Seven Natural Wonders of the World and a UNESCO World Heritage site. The Great Barrier Reef is a popular destination for snorkelers and scuba divers who come to explore its vibrant coral formations and colorful fish. However, the reef is facing numerous threats, including climate change, pollution, and overfishing, which are causing coral bleaching and the loss of marine biodiversity. Conservation efforts are underway to protect and preserve this natural wonder for future generations.

The highest waterfall in the world is Angel Falls.

Located in Venezuela's Canaima National Park, Angel Falls is the highest waterfall in the world, plunging down an impressive 3,212 feet (979 meters) from its highest point. This breathtaking natural wonder is named after American aviator Jimmie Angel, who was the first to fly over the falls in 1933. Angel Falls is not easily accessible and can only be reached by river or air, adding to its allure and exclusivity. Visitors who make the journey to see the falls are rewarded with stunning views of the cascading water, surrounded by lush tropical rainforest. The falls are particularly impressive during the rainy season, from May to November, when the water flow is at its highest. Angel Falls is a must-see destination for nature lovers and adventure seekers alike.

Do you know what island on Earth takes the crown for being the largest of them all?

Greenland is indeed the world's largest island, covering approximately 836,300 square miles (2,166,086 square kilometers) in area. It is located in the North Atlantic and Arctic oceans and is an autonomous territory of Denmark. Despite its enormous size, Greenland has a relatively small population of around 56,000 people. The island is renowned for its stunning natural beauty, including glaciers, fjords, and wildlife such as polar bears, Arctic foxes, and whales. Greenland's ice sheet is also a significant feature, containing about 8% of the world's freshwater resources. The island's unique culture, history, and geography make it a fascinating destination for travelers and researchers alike.

Do you know which city is known as the City of Lights?

The city of Paris, France, is often called the "City of Light" because it was one of the first cities in the world to introduce street lighting on a large scale. In the late 17th century, King Louis XIV ordered the installation of thousands of street lamps throughout the city to improve public safety and to help curb crime at night. The lamps were powered by candles and oil, and they were replaced over time by gas lamps, electric lamps, and other forms of lighting. Today, the nickname "City of Light" is often associated with Paris's rich cultural and artistic heritage, as well as its dazzling cityscape and vibrant nightlife.

A runway with a road crossing.

The runway of the Gibraltar International Airport intersects with a major road, Winston Churchill Avenue, which runs through the British Overseas Territory of Gibraltar. The road runs parallel to the runway for most of its length, but it intersects at a pedestrian crossing, closed whenever an aircraft is taking off or landing. When a plane approaches, the traffic barriers are closed, and pedestrians and vehicles must wait for the plane to pass before crossing. It's a unique and unusual feature of the airport, which has become a tourist attraction in its own right. The Gibraltar International Airport is located just a few miles from the city center and serves as the main gateway to the territory, with flights to and from various destinations in Europe and North Africa.

The Amazon rainforest in South America is the largest rainforest in the world.

Covering over 2.1 million square miles, the Amazon Rainforest is located in nine countries, including Brazil, Peru, and Colombia. It is home to millions of plant and animal species, many of which are found nowhere else on Earth. It is known as the "lungs of the planet", as it produces around 20% of the world's oxygen. The Amazon River, which runs through the rainforest, is the second-longest river in the world and is home to thousands of species of fish, including the piranha and the electric eel. The Amazon Rainforest has long been a subject of scientific study and exploration, and it is crucial for maintaining the Earth's biodiversity and regulating the Earth's climate.

The Nile River is the longest river in the world.

It is located in north-eastern Africa, stretching over 4,000 miles (6,650 kilometers) from its source in Burundi to its mouth in Egypt. The Nile River is a vital source of water for the people living along its banks and is known as the "lifeblood" of Egypt. It has played a significant role in the country's history and culture, and the ancient Egyptians believed it to be a god. The Nile River is also home to many species of fish, including the Nile perch and catfish, which are important food sources for local communities. The Nile River has faced many challenges, including pollution, dam construction, and climate change, which are threatening the river's ecosystem and the livelihoods of those who depend on it.

Fact# 12

Did you know that it is possible for people to float on the surface of the Dead Sea?

The Dead Sea is one of the saltiest bodies of water in the world, with a salt concentration that is nearly 10 times saltier than seawater. Because of this high salt concentration, people can easily float on the surface of the water, which has led to the sea's nickname as the "Salt Sea." The Dead Sea is located between Jordan and Israel, and it is known for its therapeutic properties due to its high salt and mineral content. The sea's salt and mineral-rich mud is believed to have a variety of health benefits for the skin and body, and it has been used for centuries for medicinal purposes. However, the Dead Sea is also facing environmental threats, including shrinking water levels and pollution, which are affecting its delicate ecosystem.

A city located on two continents.

Istanbul is the only city in the world that spans two continents, Europe and Asia. The city is situated on both sides of the Bosporus Strait, which separates the European and Asian sides of Turkey. The European side of Istanbul is home to historic landmarks such as the Hagia Sophia, the Blue Mosque, and the Topkapi Palace, while the Asian side has a more residential and commercial character. Istanbul is a city rich in history and culture, and its location at the crossroads of two continents has made it a hub of trade and cultural exchange for centuries. Today, it is the largest city in Turkey and one of the most vibrant and cosmopolitan cities in the world.

The most common Spanish surname is Garcia.

It is widely prevalent not only in Spain but also in other Spanish-speaking countries around the world. It is estimated that more than 3% of the Spanish population bears the Garcia surname, and it is also popular in Latin America, the United States, and other countries with significant Hispanic populations. The origins of the name are uncertain, but it is believed to have originated from the Basque region in northern Spain. The Garcia surname is a testament to Spain's complex and diverse history and its various cultural influences, including the Visigoths, Moors, and other peoples who have inhabited the Iberian Peninsula over the centuries.

Do you know which is the world's largest coffee producer country?

Brazil is currently the world's largest coffee producer, accounting for approximately one-third of global coffee production. The country's favorable climate and large land area suitable for coffee cultivation have contributed to its dominant position in the coffee industry. Brazil is known for producing high-quality Arabica coffee, which is widely sought after by coffee roasters and consumers around the world. The coffee industry is a significant part of Brazil's economy, providing employment and income for millions of people.

The world's oldest continuously inhabited city is Damascus.

While you might have assumed that the title of the oldest city in the world belonged to Jerusalem or Athens, it is actually Damascus, Syria, that holds this distinction. Damascus has been continuously inhabited for over 11,000 years, making it one of the oldest cities in the world. In recognition of its cultural significance, it was named the Arab Capital of Culture in 2008. The city boasts more than 125 monuments that showcase its rich history dating back to the 3rd millennium B.C., including the Great Mosque of the Umayyads, which was constructed in the 8th century. Today, Damascus is home to a population of around 1.7 million people.

Time Zones in Russia.

Russia has 11 time zones, which is the most of any country in the world. The country spans across vast distances, covering 11% of the world's land area, from the borders of Western Europe to the Pacific Ocean. As a result, different regions of Russia experience significant differences in daylight hours and seasons. The time zones are established to accommodate the large geographic area of the country and to help synchronize the business and daily routines across different regions. The practice of daylight saving time is also observed in Russia, except in some regions where it has been abolished.

The largest sand beach in world.

The largest sand beach in the world is located in Australia, specifically on Fraser Island, which is also the largest island made entirely of sand. Fraser Island is situated on the east coast of Australia and measures approximately 76.4 miles in length and 13.6 miles in width. The beach on Fraser Island is known as the "75-Mile Beach" due to its impressive length, and it is a popular tourist destination for visitors to the area.

The beach on Fraser Island is unique due to its pure, white sand that is made up entirely of quartz crystals. The sand is so fine that it squeaks when walked on, and it is also relatively cool, even on hot summer days. Visitors to the island can enjoy a variety of activities on the beach, including swimming, fishing, and sunbathing.

The amazing location of Africa.

Africa is situated in all four hemispheres – northern, southern, eastern, and western. The equator passes through the central region of the continent, dividing it into the northern and southern hemispheres. Additionally, the Prime Meridian, which is the line of longitude that marks 0 degrees and separates the eastern and western hemispheres, passes through the continent in the western part of Africa. As a result of its location in all four hemispheres, Africa experiences a wide range of climatic conditions and is home to a diverse array of ecosystems and species. From the deserts of the Sahara in the north to the tropical rainforests of the Congo Basin in the center, and the savannas and grasslands of the south, Africa's geography is complex and varied.

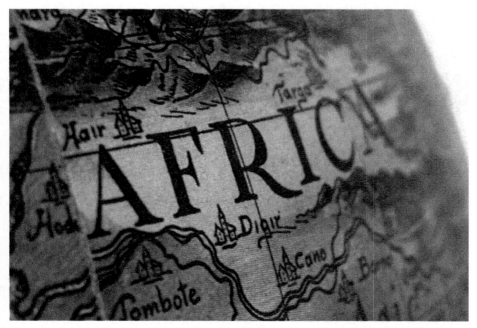

Mexico city is sinking.

Mexico City is sinking at an alarming rate of 4 to 6 inches per year, which is attributed to its construction over a former lake bed. Over the last six decades, the city has sunk almost 10 meters (or 32 feet), which poses a significant risk to its infrastructure, including buildings, roads, and other essential services. The city's rapid urbanization and increasing demand for water have resulted in over-extraction of groundwater from the underlying aquifer, which exacerbates the problem of land subsidence. The government is implementing various measures to reduce water consumption, promote sustainable development, and improve infrastructure resilience. However, the ongoing population growth and other socio-economic factors may complicate these efforts.

First city to reach one million residents.

Rome was the first city in the world to reach a population of one million inhabitants back in 133 BC, while London and New York followed suit in 1810 and 1875, respectively. Fast forward to today, and there are over 300 cities worldwide with more than one million inhabitants. This exponential growth in urbanization is a reflection of the significant demographic shifts that have occurred worldwide. With the increasing trend toward urbanization, cities continue to play an essential role in shaping economies, cultures, and societies around the globe. However, this unprecedented growth has also brought about significant challenges, including urban sprawl, infrastructure deficits, and social and economic inequalities.

An Island where the owner countries switch every six months.

Pheasant Island, located in the Bidassoa River, is unique as it changes sovereignty between Spain and France every six months. Spain exercises control over the island for the first half of the year, while France takes over the island for the remaining six months. This tradition dates back to the 17th century when the island served as a neutral meeting place for the signing of a peace treaty between the two countries. Today, the island remains a symbol of the peaceful coexistence and diplomatic relations between France and Spain. However, the island is generally not open to the public and remains a strictly controlled area due to its strategic location on the border between the two countries.

Have you ever heard about snowfall in the Sahara Desert?

The Sahara desert, located in Africa, is the largest hot desert on earth. Despite its scorching temperatures, an extraordinary event occurred on 18 February 1979 when the desert experienced a rare snowfall. This marked the first time that the low latitude zones of the Sahara recorded snowfall. The snow fell for almost half an hour in Southern Algeria, leading to a snowstorm that caused traffic disruptions. The unusual phenomenon was attributed to a combination of factors, including a cold air mass that moved across the region and an unusual low-pressure system that caused the cold air to descend towards the ground. This unusual occurrence serves as a reminder that the earth's weather patterns can be unpredictable and can bring about unexpected events even in the most extreme environments.

There is a mountain taller than Mount Everest.

Mount Everest is widely known as the highest mountain in the world above sea level, standing tall at 8,848 meters or 29,028 feet. However, a fascinating fact is that the tallest mountains in the United States are not the Rockies or the Sierra Nevada but Mauna Kea of Hawaii, which measures more than 32,000 feet from its base on the seafloor. Despite this, only 13,798 feet of Mauna Kea extends above sea level, with the remaining base being submerged under the sea level. Despite its impressive height, Mauna Kea does not receive the same level of recognition and hype as the Himalayas, which may be attributed to its location on a remote island in the Pacific Ocean.

Fact# 25

Russian and US borders are both reachable on foot.

During certain times of the year, it is theoretically possible to travel on foot from the United States to Russia via the two Diomede Islands. Big Diomede Island is located in Russia, while Little Diomede Island is part of the state of Alaska in the United States. These two islands are separated by the International Date Line and the Bering Strait, which is a narrow body of water that separates Asia from North America. In winter, the water between these two islands can freeze over, creating a temporary land bridge that would allow people to walk between them. However, this journey can be extremely dangerous due to the harsh weather conditions, unpredictable sea ice, and strong currents in the Bering Strait.

Netherland is famous for tulips.

Tulips are indeed one of the Netherlands' most iconic symbols and have been an essential part of Dutch culture for centuries. Tulips were first introduced to the Netherlands in the late 16th century from the Ottoman Empire, and they quickly became popular among the wealthy elite as a status symbol. In the 17th century, the tulip trade reached its peak, and the period is known as "tulip mania." The tulip season typically runs from March to May; the famous tulip fields can be seen in full bloom during this time. The Keukenhof Gardens, located in Lisse, is one of the most popular tourist destinations in the Netherlands during the tulip season, attracting millions of visitors each year.

The unknown soldier lies beneath Arc de Triomphe, France.

The Unknown Soldier under the Arc de Triomphe in Paris, France, represents all the French soldiers who died in World War I and were never identified. The soldier was interred there on Armistice Day, November 11, 1920, in a ceremony presided over by French Prime Minister Georges Clemenceau. The tomb is inscribed with the words, "Here lies a French soldier who died for the fatherland 1914–1918," it serves as a reminder of the sacrifice made by so many during the war. In 1921, an eternal flame was lit on top of the tomb to symbolize the memory of the Unknown Soldier and all those who gave their lives for France. Today, the Arc de Triomphe and the Tomb of the Unknown Soldier are essential symbols of French national identity and a popular destination for visitors to Paris.

One of the US states was bought by US from Russia.

It was Alaska, bought by US from Russia in 1867. The purchase was known as the Alaska Purchase or the Treaty of Cession, and it was negotiated by U.S. Secretary of State William Seward and Russian Minister to the United States Eduard de Stoeckl. The United States paid Russia $7.2 million for the territory, which many viewed as a barren, frozen wasteland at the time. However, the discovery of gold and other valuable resources in Alaska soon changed that perception and the state became an important part of the United States economically and strategically. Today, Alaska is the largest state in the United States by land area and is known for its stunning natural beauty, abundant wildlife, and unique culture.

The world's highest capital city.

The world's highest capital city is La Paz, Bolivia. It is located at an elevation of around 3,650 meters (11,975 feet) above sea level, which makes it the highest administrative capital in the world. The city's metropolitan area has a population of around 2.3 million people, making it one of the largest urban areas in Bolivia. Despite its high altitude, La Paz has a mild climate due to its location near the equator. The city's location in the Andean valley also provides stunning views of the surrounding mountains and natural scenery. La Paz is known for its rich cultural heritage, and its historic downtown area is a UNESCO World Heritage site. The city has numerous museums, art galleries, and cultural centers, showcasing Bolivia's indigenous heritage and colonial history.

The country with most Islands on earth.

Indonesia has the most islands of any country in the world. Indonesia is an archipelago country located in Southeast Asia and Oceania, consisting of more than 17,000 islands. The largest islands in Indonesia are Java, Sumatra, Borneo (shared with Malaysia and Brunei), Sulawesi, and New Guinea (shared with Papua New Guinea). Indonesia also has many smaller islands, including Bali, Lombok, and the Gili Islands, which are popular tourist destinations. The diverse geography of Indonesia, which includes tropical forests, coral reefs, mountains, and volcanoes, makes it one of the most biodiverse countries in the world, with many unique plant and animal species.

A country in Asia has a unique flag.

Nepal has a unique flag that is different from most other national flags in the world. It is the only national flag in the world that is not rectangular or square in shape. The flag of Nepal is a combination of two pennants, or triangular flags, stacked on top of each other. The upper pennant is white and represents the Himalayan mountains and the snowy peaks of Nepal. The lower pennant is red and represents the courage and passion of the Nepalese people. The two pennants are joined together at a common diagonal line, which represents the upliftment of the country and the desire for peace. The current design of the flag was adopted in 1962, although similar designs have been used by Nepalese rulers for centuries.

The brightest man-made place on earth.

The brightest man-made place on Earth, when viewed from space, is the city of Las Vegas, Nevada, in the United States. The city's bright lights, including the famous Las Vegas Strip with its numerous casinos, hotels, and other attractions, make it easily visible from space. The reason for the city's brightness is due to the large number of neon lights, LED signs, and other lighting fixtures that are used to illuminate the city at night. The lights are so bright that they can be seen from over 10 miles above the Earth's surface, making Las Vegas one of the most recognizable landmarks when viewed from space. However, it is worth noting that there are other cities and areas on Earth that are also very bright when viewed from space, including other major metropolitan areas such as Tokyo, New York City, and Shanghai.

Fact# 33

Tallest people in the world.

The Netherlands is known for having some of the tallest people in the world; on average, Dutch men are among the tallest in the world. According to data from the World Health Organization (WHO), the average height for adult Dutch men is approximately 1.83 meters (6 feet), which is higher than the global average height for men. There are many factors that contribute to the height of the Dutch population, including genetics, diet, and lifestyle. Dutch people tend to have a diet high in dairy products, which are rich in calcium and other nutrients vital for bone growth and development. They also tend to have high levels of physical activity, which can help to promote healthy growth and development.

Earth's largest and most populous continent.

The largest and most populous continent on Earth is Asia. It covers an area of approximately 44.5 million square kilometers (17.2 million square miles), which is about 30% of the total land area of the Earth, and it is home to more than 4.6 billion people, which is over 60% of the world's population. Asia is a diverse continent that includes many different countries, cultures, languages, and religions. Some of the largest countries in Asia by area include Russia, China, India, and Kazakhstan, while some of the most populous countries include China, India, Indonesia, and Pakistan. The continent of Asia is also home to some of the world's largest and most iconic landmarks, including the Great Wall of China, the Taj Mahal in India, the Petronas Towers in Malaysia, and the Burj Khalifa in Dubai.

The country with the highest number of venomous snakes in the world.

Australia is known to have the highest number of venomous snakes of any country in the world. Of the 3,000 species of snakes found worldwide, around 170 of them are found in Australia, and approximately 100 of those are venomous. Some of the most venomous snakes in Australia include the inland taipan, which has the most potent venom of any snake in the world, the eastern brown snake, the coastal taipan, the tiger snake, and the death adder. While encounters with venomous snakes in Australia are relatively rare, it is still important to take precautions when exploring the Australian wilderness or visiting areas where snakes are known to be present.

New York was originally called New Amsterdam.

New York City was originally founded by the Dutch in 1624 as a fur trading post called New Amsterdam. The settlement was located on the southern tip of Manhattan Island, which the Dutch named Nieuw Amsterdam after the city of Amsterdam in the Netherlands. In 1664, the English captured New Amsterdam from the Dutch and renamed it New York after the Duke of York, the brother of King Charles II of England. The English renamed the entire colony of New Netherlands, which included parts of present-day New York, New Jersey, Connecticut, Delaware, and Pennsylvania, as the Province of New York. Today, many reminders of New York City's Dutch heritage can still be found in the city, such as street names (e.g. Wall Street, Broadway), the architecture of some buildings, and the influence of Dutch culture on the city's art, food, and traditions.

The shortest national anthem in the world.

The Japanese national anthem, "Kimigayo," is the shortest national anthem in the world, with only four lines of text. The anthem has been in use in its current form since the late 19th century, although its origins can be traced back to much earlier periods of Japanese history. The lyrics of "Kimigayo" are written in classical Japanese and are based on a poem from the Heian period (794-1185) that was often used to honor the emperor. The anthem's text translates to: "May your reign Continue for a thousand, eight thousand generations Until the pebbles Grow into boulders Lush with moss." While "Kimigayo" has been controversial at times due to its associations with Japan's imperial past and wartime history, it remains an important symbol of national identity and pride for many Japanese people.

National Anthem without lyrics.

The Spanish national anthem, "Marcha Real" (Royal March), has no official lyrics. The march has been used as the national anthem of Spain since the 18th century, although it was not officially adopted as such until 1997. Despite its lack of lyrics, "Marcha Real" is widely recognized as the national anthem of Spain and is played at official events, such as state ceremonies, military parades, and sporting events. Interestingly, the lack of lyrics to the Spanish national anthem is somewhat unusual among national anthems. Most national anthems have lyrics meant to express patriotic sentiments and honor the history and culture of the country. However, a few other national anthems, such as the national anthem of San Marino, also do not have any official lyrics.

Do you know which is the Largest country in the world?

Russia is the largest country in the world by land area, with a total area of approximately 17.1 million square kilometers (6.6 million square miles). It spans two continents, Europe and Asia, and borders several countries, including China, Kazakhstan, Mongolia, and Ukraine. Russia's vast land area includes a wide range of geographic features, from the far north's frozen tundra to the west's fertile plains and the south's mountain ranges. It is also home to diverse flora and fauna, including Siberian tigers, brown bears, and reindeer. Despite its size, Russia's population is relatively small compared to other countries, with a population of approximately 144 million. The country's capital and largest city is Moscow, which is located in the western part of the country.

Fact# 40

Smallest country in the world.

The smallest country in the world is Vatican City, also known as the Holy See. It is an independent city-state enclaved within Rome, Italy, and has a total area of only 44 hectares (110 acres), making it the smallest country in the world by land area and population. Vatican City is the spiritual and administrative center of the Roman Catholic Church, and it is home to many important religious sites, including St. Peter's Basilica, the Sistine Chapel, and the Vatican Museums. The Pope, who is the leader of the Catholic Church, is also the head of state of Vatican City. Despite its small size, Vatican City is a highly influential and well-known entity on the global stage. It maintains diplomatic relations with many countries worldwide and is often involved in international affairs, particularly religion and human rights.

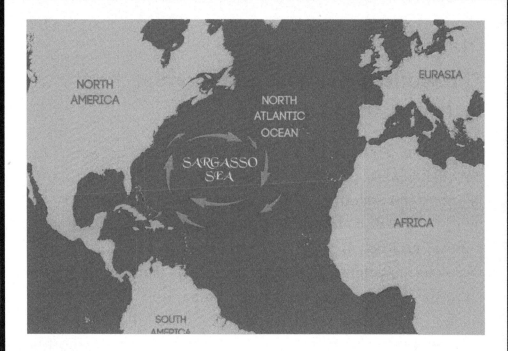

The Sargasso Sea is the only one without coasts.

The Sargasso Sea is a region of the North Atlantic Ocean that is bounded by several ocean currents, including the Gulf Stream, the North Atlantic Current, the Canary Current, and the West Atlantic Equatorial Current. While land-based coasts do not technically surround the Sargasso Sea, it is still connected to the surrounding ocean and bordered by various countries' exclusive economic zones. The Sargasso Sea is named after the Sargassum seaweed that floats on its surface, and it is known for its unique ecosystem that includes a diverse array of marine life, including various species of fish, sea turtles, and birds. The region is also crucial for ocean research due to its distinctive oceanic conditions and the presence of a large concentration of microplastics.

The world's shortest commercial flight lasts less than a minute.

The world's shortest commercial flight is between the Scottish islands of Westray and Papa Westray in the Orkney Islands. The distance between the two islands is just 1.7 miles (2.7 kilometers), and the flight takes less than a minute, typically around 35 seconds. Loganair operates the flight and is primarily used by locals for medical and other essential travel. However, it has also become a popular tourist attraction, with visitors taking the flight to experience the unique thrill of one of the world's shortest commercial flights. Despite its short duration, the flight still follows standard aviation safety procedures, including pre-flight safety checks and the use of a flight attendant.

Bangkok's full name is 163 Letters.

Bangkok's full ceremonial name is one of the longest city names in the world, with 169 letters in the Thai language. However, it is commonly abbreviated to a shorter version for everyday use. The full ceremonial name of Bangkok in Thai is **"กรุงเทพมหานคร อมรรัตนโกสินทร์ มหินทรายุธยา มหาดิลกภพ นพรัตนราชธานีบูรีรมย์ อุดมราชนิเวศน์มหาสถาน อมรพิมานอวตาร สถิต สังขะวงศ์วังเหนือ"**. The English translation of Bangkok's full ceremonial name is "The city of angels, the great city, the eternal jewel city, the impregnable city of God Indra, the grand capital of the world endowed with nine precious gems, the happy city, abounding in an enormous Royal Palace that resembles the heavenly abode where reigns the reincarnated god, a city given by Indra and built by Vishnukarn".

Fact# 44

The coldest temperature ever recorded was −128.6°F (−89.2°C).

The coldest temperature ever recorded on Earth was −128.6°F (−89.2°C) at the Soviet Union's Vostok Station in Antarctica on July 21, 1983. This temperature was measured using satellite observations and is recognized as Earth's lowest reliably measured temperature. Antarctica is known for its extreme cold temperatures, with many regions experiencing average temperatures well below freezing throughout the year. The cold temperatures are due to several factors, including the high latitude of the continent, the polar climate, and the continent's isolation from warmer ocean currents. While the extreme cold of Antarctica can be dangerous for humans, it is also a unique and fascinating region with its own distinct ecosystem, including penguins, seals, and various species of marine life that have adapted to the harsh conditions.

The hottest temperature ever recorded on earth is 134°F (56.7°C).

The hottest temperature ever reliably recorded on Earth was 134°F (56.7°C) at Furnace Creek Ranch in Death Valley, California, USA, on July 10, 1913. This temperature was measured by a weather station located at the ranch and has been recognized as Earth's highest reliably measured temperature. Death Valley is known for its extreme heat, with many regions experiencing average temperatures above 100°F (38°C) during summer. The high temperatures are due to several factors, including the low elevation of the region, the arid desert climate, and the presence of mountains that trap hot air. It's worth noting that there have been reports of even higher temperatures in other parts of the world, but these readings have not been verified or confirmed by reliable sources.

The longest international border.

The border between Canada and the United States is the world's longest international border, stretching over 8,891 kilometers (5,525 miles) from the Atlantic Ocean in the east to the Pacific Ocean in the west. The border is primarily defined by the 49th parallel, which separates the two countries for much of its length, although there are also several other sections where the border follows natural features such as rivers and lakes. The Canada–US border has played an important role in the relationship between the two countries, serving as a symbol of their long-standing friendship and peaceful coexistence, as well as facilitating trade, tourism, and cultural exchange between the two nations.

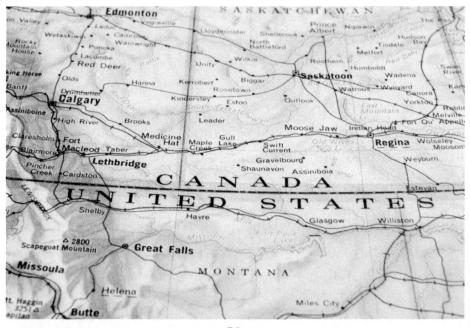

The longest wall on earth.

The Great Wall of China is the world's longest wall, stretching for around 13,170 miles (21,196 kilometers) across northern China. Construction on the wall began in the 7th century BCE and continued for centuries until the Ming dynasty completed its final phase in the 16th century CE. Its primary purpose was to defend China against various nomadic groups from the north. The wall is made up of various materials, including brick, tamped earth, stone, and wood. In addition to its military function, the Great Wall has become an iconic symbol of Chinese civilization and culture. Today, it is a major tourist attraction and a testament to the resilience and determination of the people who built it.

Fact# 48

There is no mosquito in Iceland.

Iceland is known for its pristine landscapes, geothermal hot springs, and unique wildlife, but one thing it doesn't have is mosquitoes. Despite its cool and damp climate, Iceland lacks mosquitoes due to a combination of factors, including its isolation from other land masses, unfavorable weather conditions for mosquito breeding, and the absence of native mosquito species. This makes Iceland a popular destination for travelers who want to avoid the nuisance of mosquito bites while enjoying the country's natural beauty. However, while Iceland may be mosquito-free, it is important to remember that other insects, such as midges and ticks, can still be found in certain areas and may pose a risk to human health.

Yellowstone national park is home to a Supervolcano.

Yellowstone National Park is located above a supervolcano that has the potential to cause a catastrophic eruption. The Yellowstone Caldera, which is the crater formed by the last major eruption of the supervolcano, measures approximately 30 miles (48 kilometers) by 45 miles (72 kilometers) and is one of the largest active volcanic systems in the world. However, it is important to note that the probability of a significant eruption occurring soon is relatively low. The last major eruption at Yellowstone occurred approximately 640,000 years ago, and the volcanic activity in the region has been relatively calm since then.

The deepest place on Earth.

The Mariana Trench, located in the Pacific Ocean, is the deepest place on Earth, with a maximum depth of approximately 36,070 feet (10,994 meters). It is located in the western Pacific, east of the Mariana Islands, and is part of the larger Mariana Trench system, which includes several other deep subduction zones. The Mariana Trench is known for its extreme conditions, including high pressures, low temperatures, and limited sunlight. Despite these challenges, the trench is home to a variety of unique and adapted species, including giant amphipods, deep-sea jellyfish, and other creatures that have evolved to survive in the extreme environment. The first recorded descent to the bottom of the Mariana Trench was in 1960 by the bathyscaphe Trieste, piloted by Jacques Piccard and Don Walsh.

The Leaning Tower of Pisa was built over a period of almost 200 years.

Its construction was started in the 12th century and continued until the 14th century. It is also known as the "Torre pendente di Pisa" in Italian. The tower is located in the Italian city of Pisa, in the Tuscany region. The tower is famous for its distinctive lean, caused by an uneven foundation that was not properly accounted for during its construction. The tower stands at approximately 56 meters (184 feet) tall and leans at an angle of about 3.97 degrees. In recent years, efforts have been made to stabilize the tower and prevent it from leaning further or toppling over. Despite its lean, the Leaning Tower of Pisa remains one of Italy's most popular tourist attractions and is visited by millions of people each year.

A country with the most spoken languages.

Papua New Guinea is a country located in the southwestern Pacific Ocean and is known for having the most spoken languages of any country in the world. It is estimated that there are over 800 different languages spoken in Papua New Guinea, accounting for about 12% of the world's total number of languages. The reason for this incredible linguistic diversity in Papua New Guinea is due to its geography and history. The country is made up of over 600 islands, many of which are isolated from one another by rugged terrain, dense forests, and high mountains. Over time, this isolation has led to the development of distinct languages and dialects in different regions of the country.
Furthermore, Papua New Guinea is home to a large number of indigenous ethnic groups, each with its own unique cultural and linguistic traditions.

The closest peak to outer space is not Mount Everest it is Chimborazo.

Chimborazo is a dormant stratovolcano located in the Andes mountain range of Ecuador. While it is not the tallest mountain in the world (it stands at 6,263 meters or 20,548 feet), it is considered the "closest" peak to outer space. This is because of a phenomenon called the "geoid effect," which causes the Earth's equatorial bulge to push the surface farther away from the planet's center at the equator than at the poles. As a result, Chimborazo's summit is actually farther away from the Earth's center than the summit of Mount Everest, even though Everest is taller. In fact, if you measure from the Earth's center rather than from sea level, Chimborazo's peak is the farthest point from the center of the planet. As a result, the summit of Chimborazo is considered to be the point on Earth closest to outer space, as measured from the center of the planet.

America's first capital wasn't Washington, D.C.

The United States's first capital was located in New York City. After the American Revolution, the newly formed United States had to establish a capital city where the government could meet and conduct business. In 1785, the Continental Congress established its capital in New York City, the largest city in the country and a major center of commerce and politics. However, the capital was later moved to Philadelphia, Pennsylvania, where it remained until 1800. It was not until 1800 that the capital was finally forced to its current location of Washington, D.C., which was explicitly created as the new capital city of the United States.

The shortest place name in the world is Å.

Å is a village in the municipality of Moskenes, in the county of Nordland, Norway. It is located on the western coast of the Lofoten Islands and has a population of around 100 people. The village's name is derived from the Old Norse word "á", which means "river." The letter "Å" is also used in the Norwegian and Swedish alphabets and represents a long "o" sound. The name Å is often used to symbolize Scandinavian culture and is a popular tourist destination for its scenic landscapes, fishing, and outdoor activities. Despite its small size and short name, Å has a rich history and cultural heritage that attracts visitors from all over the world.

Only one country in the Caribbean has railway system.

Cuba is the only country in the Caribbean that has a railway system. The railway in Cuba was first established in the 19th century during the Spanish colonial period and was later expanded during the early 20th century under American influence. The railway played an important role in the transportation of goods and people throughout the country, connecting major cities and towns. Today, the Cuban railway system is operated by the state-owned company Ferrocarriles de Cuba and provides transportation for both passengers and freight. While the railway system in Cuba is not as extensive as it once was, it remains an important part of the country's transportation infrastructure and a unique feature of the Caribbean region.

Fact# 57

Airplanes are not allowed to fly over the Taj Mahal.

The restriction on air traffic over the Taj Mahal was imposed to protect the monument from pollution and environmental damage caused by aircraft emissions. The ban was put in place in 2001 by the Indian government and applies to all aircraft, including commercial and private planes. In addition to the ban on overflights, there are also restrictions on vehicular traffic in the vicinity of the Taj Mahal to minimize pollution and preserve the beauty and integrity of the site. These measures demonstrate the Indian government's commitment to protecting its cultural and natural heritage for future generations to enjoy.

The longest mountain range in the world is the Andes in South America

The Andes mountain range is located in South America and is the longest mountain range in the world, stretching over 7,000 kilometers (4,300 miles) along the western coast of the continent. The Andes span through seven countries: Venezuela, Colombia, Ecuador, Peru, Bolivia, Chile, and Argentina, and are home to many diverse ecosystems and indigenous cultures. The highest peak in the Andes is Aconcagua, which is located in Argentina and stands at an elevation of 6,960 meters (22,837 feet). The Andes are an important source of natural resources, including minerals and water, and are a popular destination for outdoor enthusiasts who come to hike, climb, and explore the diverse landscapes and cultures of the region.

The world's deadliest earthquake in history.

The deadliest earthquake in recorded history occurred in central China on January 23, 1556, during the Ming Dynasty. The earthquake had an estimated magnitude of 8.0 on the Richter scale and killed approximately 830,000 people. The earthquake was so powerful that it destroyed many cities and villages and was felt over an area of more than 2.2 million square kilometers (850,000 square miles). The exact number of casualties is difficult to determine due to the lack of accurate record-keeping during that time, but it is considered one of the deadliest natural disasters in human history. The earthquake profoundly impacted Chinese society and culture and has been the subject of many literary and artistic works throughout the centuries.

The country with the most neighbouring countries.

The country with the most neighboring countries is China, which shares borders with 14 other countries. China is located in East Asia and is the world's most populous country, with a population of over 1.4 billion people. Its neighboring countries include Russia, Mongolia, Kazakhstan, Kyrgyzstan, Tajikistan, Afghanistan, Pakistan, India, Nepal, Bhutan, Myanmar, Laos, Vietnam, and North Korea. The diverse geography and cultures of China and its neighboring countries have influenced each other over centuries and continue to shape the region's politics, economy, and social dynamics. China's extensive borders have played a significant role in its history, shaping its interactions with neighboring nations and influencing the development of its culture and civilization.

Continents shift at about the same rate as your fingernails grow.

The movement of Earth's tectonic plates, which are the large pieces of the Earth's crust that make up the continents, is called plate tectonics. The rate of plate movement is relatively slow, occurring at a rate of about 2-3 centimeters (0.8-1.2 inches) per year, which is roughly the same rate that human fingernails grow. This may seem slow, but over the course of millions of years, the movement of the plates can significantly impact the Earth's surface and the distribution of its land masses. Plate tectonics is responsible for many geological phenomena, such as earthquakes, volcanic eruptions, and the formation of mountain ranges, and has played a crucial role in shaping the Earth's history and evolution.

The largest country in the world by land area is Russia.

It covers approximately 6.6 million square miles (17.1 million square kilometers), which is more than one-eighth of the Earth's land area. Russia spans across two continents, Europe and Asia, and has a diverse range of landscapes, including vast forests, expansive grasslands, and rugged mountains. Its population is around 144 million, making it the ninth most populous country in the world. It is also home to several iconic landmarks, including St. Basil's Cathedral in Moscow, the Hermitage Museum in St. Petersburg, and Lake Baikal, the deepest lake in the world. Russia's economy is largely based on its natural resources, such as oil, natural gas, and minerals, which are found in abundance throughout the country.

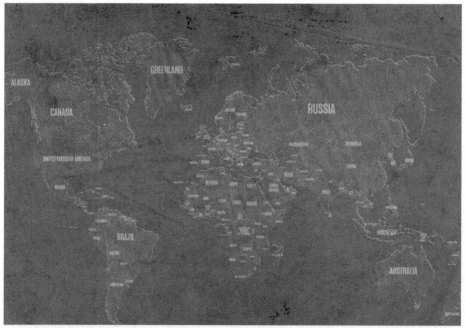

The driest place on Earth.

The Atacama Desert in South America is the driest place on Earth, receiving an average rainfall of just 0.04 inches (1 millimeter) per year. The Atacama Desert is located along the Pacific coast of Chile and extends into Peru, Bolivia, and Argentina. It is known for its arid, barren landscape and is often used as a location for testing and developing space technology due to its similarities to the surface of Mars. Despite its extreme conditions, the Atacama Desert is home to a variety of plant and animal species, including the llama and the vicuña, a South American camelid. The Atacama Desert is also a popular destination for stargazing, as its clear, dry air and high altitude make it an ideal location for observing the night sky.

Fact# 64

The largest group of fresh water.

The Great Lakes, located in North America, are the largest group of freshwater lakes in the world, containing 21% of the world's fresh water. The Great Lakes consist of five interconnected lakes, including Lake Superior, Lake Michigan, Lake Huron, Lake Erie, and Lake Ontario, located on the border between the United States and Canada. The lakes are a vital resource for drinking water, shipping, and recreation and play an essential role in the region's economy and ecology. The Great Lakes are home to various fish species, including lake trout, salmon, and walleye, and support numerous plant and animal species that depend on the lakes for their survival.

The place on earth with the most active volcanoes and earthquakes.

The Ring of Fire, a horseshoe-shaped area around the Pacific Ocean, is home to 75% of the world's active and dormant volcanoes and 90% of the world's earthquakes. The Ring of Fire is approximately 25,000 miles (40,000 kilometers) long and encompasses numerous countries, including Japan, Indonesia, Chile, and the United States. The intense volcanic and seismic activity in the Ring of Fire is due to the collision of several tectonic plates, which create pressure and friction that can cause earthquakes and volcanic eruptions. While the Ring of Fire is known for its destructive potential, it is also a source of geothermal energy and mineral resources and is home to unique ecosystems that have adapted to the extreme conditions.

The coldest, driest and windiest continent.

Antarctica, the fifth-largest continent, is the coldest, driest, and windiest continent on Earth, with an average temperature of -56°C (-68°F). Antarctica is located at the southernmost point on the globe and is covered in ice that averages 1 mile (1.6 kilometers) in thickness. Despite its harsh conditions, Antarctica is home to a variety of wildlife, including penguins, seals, and whales, that have adapted to the extreme environment. Antarctica also plays an important role in the Earth's climate system, as the ice sheets and glaciers store approximately 70% of the planet's freshwater. Antarctic research has also led to important discoveries in fields such as geology, biology, and climate science.

THANK YOU

We express our sincere gratitude for taking the time to read our book on Geography interesting facts. We hope it has provided you with a wealth of knowledge and insights into the fascinating world of geography.

We want to thank our readers for their continued support and enthusiasm for this book. Without your encouragement, this book would not have been possible. We would also like to thank our team of researchers, writers, editors, and designers who worked tirelessly to bring this book to life. Their hard work and dedication have been invaluable in making this project successful.

Lastly, we want to extend our gratitude to the incredible planet we live on. The wonders of nature and the complex systems that sustain life continue to inspire us and fuel our curiosity about the world.

Once again, thank you for choosing to read our book. We hope it has sparked your interest in geography and inspired you to learn more about the amazing planet we call home.

Thank you for choosing and trusting us!

Don't forget to share your experience and give a review.

sharpmindslearning.com

Printed in Great Britain
by Amazon

32441675R00046